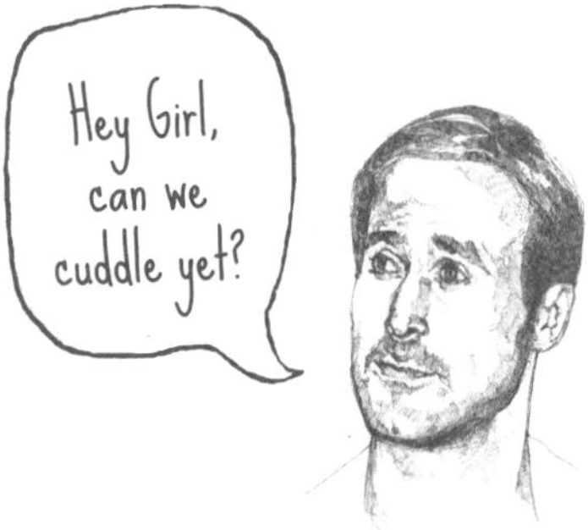
Hey Girl,
can we
cuddle yet?

Hey Girl, who cares what they think? Just be yourself.

Hey Girl,
who cares what
they think? Just
be yourself.

Hey Girl,

Hey Girl,
who cares what
they think? Just
be yourself.

Hey Girl, who cares what they think? Just be yourself.

Hey Girl,
who cares what
they think? Just
be yourself.

Hey Girl,

Hey Girl,
who cares what
they think? Just
be yourself.

Hey Girl,

Hey Girl, who cares what they think? Just be yourself.

Hey Girl,

Hey Girl,
who cares what
they think? Just
be yourself.

Hey Girl,

Hey Girl,

Hey Girl,
who cares what
they think? Just
be yourself.

Hey Girl,
who cares what
they think? Just
be yourself.

Hey Girl,

Hey Girl, who cares what they think? Just be yourself.

Hey Girl,

Hey Girl,
who cares what
they think? Just
be yourself.

Hey Girl,
who cares what
they think? Just
be yourself.

Hey Girl, who cares what they think? Just be yourself.

Hey Girl, tell me everything about your day.

Hey Girl,

Hey Girl, who cares what they think? Just be yourself.

Hey Girl,

Hey Girl,